Dictionary of Space

Katie Sharp

Rigby
A Harcourt Achieve Imprint

www.Rigby.com
1-800-531-5015

Astronauts

Astronauts are people who go into space.

They fly in spaceships.

Astronauts look at the planets and

the moon.

2

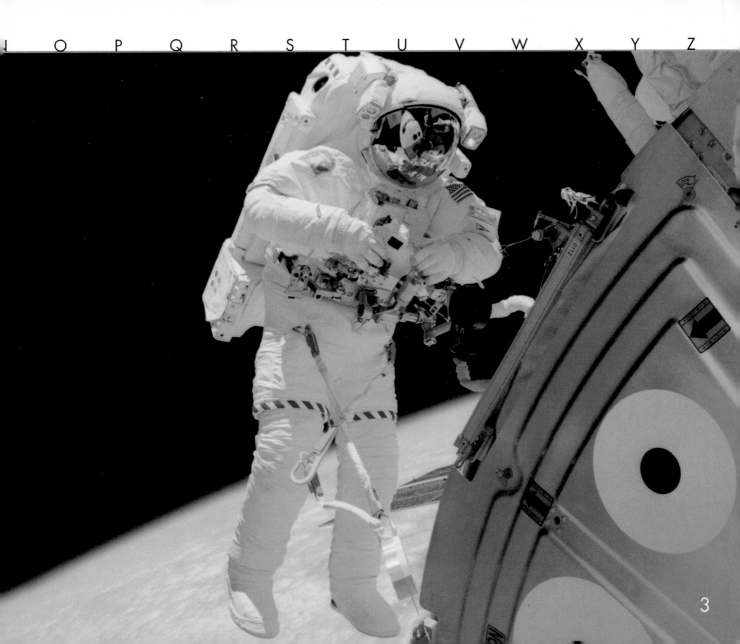

3

Comets

Comets are large balls of ice and dust in space.

We can only see comets at night.

They must be very close to the sun.

Then we see their bright, shining tails.

Earth

Earth is the place where we live.

Earth is in space.

Earth has water, land, and air.

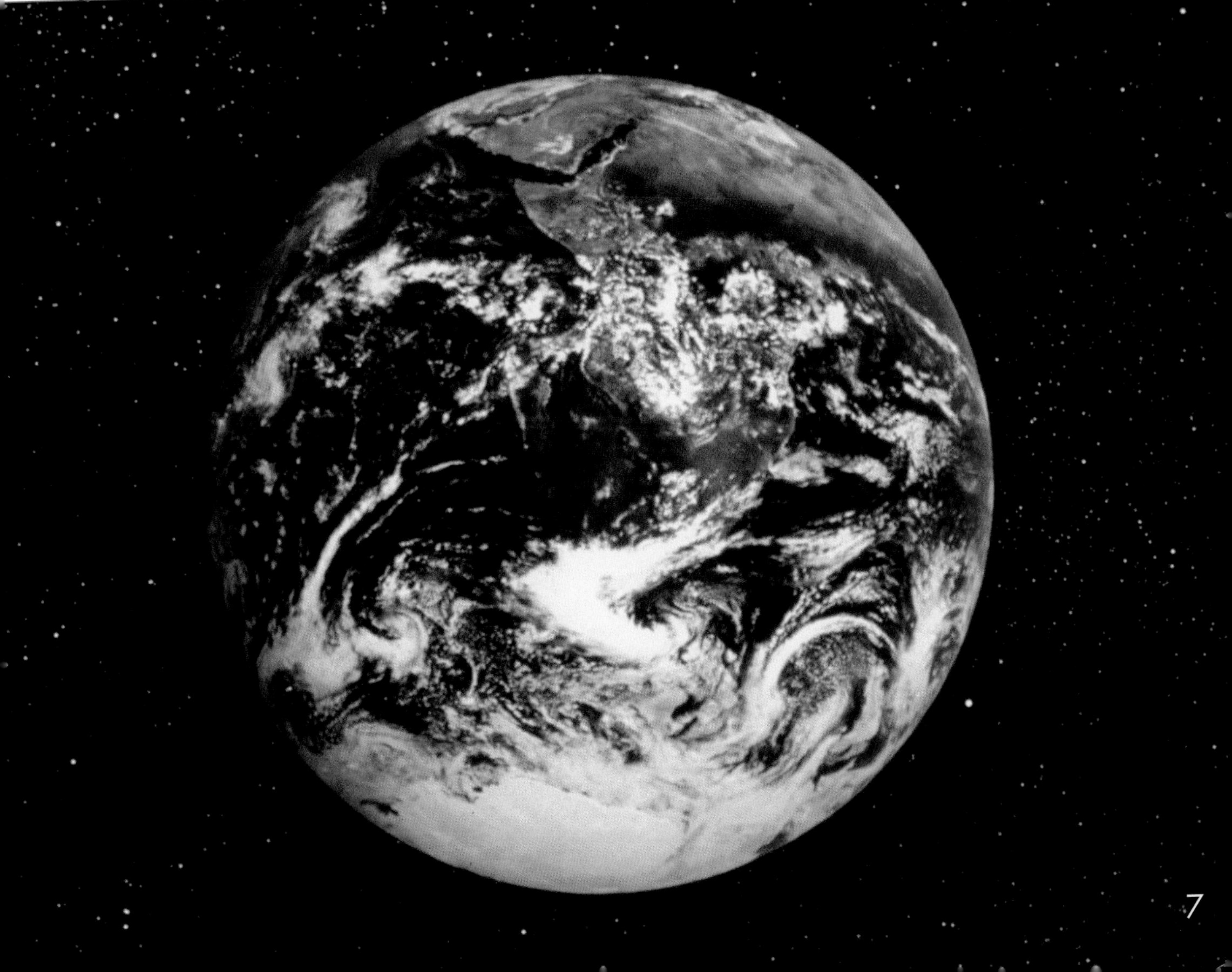

Moon

The moon is Earth's neighbor in space.

It is mostly made of rock.

No one can live there.

We can see the moon in the sky.

8

Planets

Planets are large objects in space.

They travel around the sun.

There are eight planets

in our solar system.

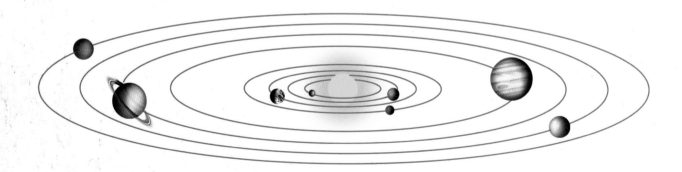

Stars

Stars are hot balls of gas.

Stars look like small dots in the sky,

but stars are very big.

They are just far away!

12

Sun

The sun is a giant star.

It is very hot.

The sun helps plants grow and keeps us warm.

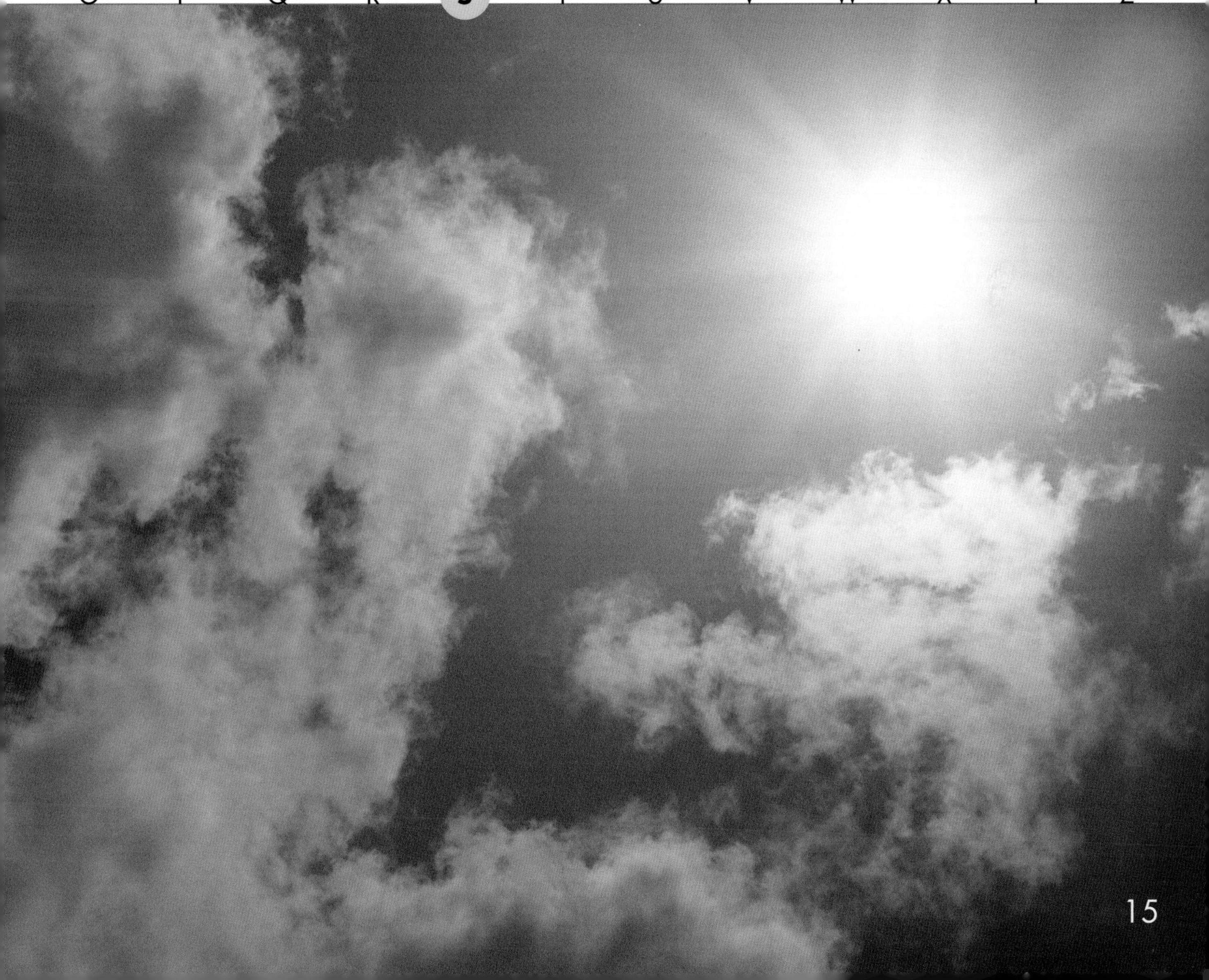

Telescope

A telescope is a tool we use
to see things in space.
It makes the moon, planets, and
stars look closer than they really are.